PINGRY SCHOOL
SHORT HILLS CAMPUS
WITHDRAWN
COUNTRY DAY DRIVE
SHORT HILLS, N. J. 07078

W9-AZR-231

DOGS

DALMATIANS

STUART A. KALLEN
ABDO & Daughters

Published by Abdo & Daughters, 4940 Viking Drive, Suite 622,
Edina, Minnesota 55435.

Library bound edition distributed by Rockbottom Books, Pentagon
Tower, P.O. Box 36036, Minneapolis, Minnesota 55435.

Copyright © 1996 by Abdo Consulting Group, Inc., Pentagon Tower,
P.O. Box 36036, Minneapolis, Minnesota 55435 USA. International
copyrights reserved in all countries. No part of this book may be
reproduced in any form without written permission from the publisher.

Printed in the United States.

Cover Photo credit: Peter Arnold, Inc.
Interior Photo credits: Peter Arnold, Inc.

Edited by Rosemary Wallner

Library of Congress Cataloging-in-Publication data

Kallen, Stuart A., 1955
Dalmatians / Stuart A. Kallen.
    p. cm. — (Dogs)
    Includes bibliographical references (p. 24) and index.
    ISBN 1-56239-455-X
1. Dalmatian dog—Juvenile literature. [1. Dalmatian dog. 2. Dogs.] I. Title. II.
Series Kallen, Stuart A.,   1955- Dogs.
SF429.D3K35 1995
636.7'2—dc20   95-4019
                                                              CIP
                                                              AC

ABOUT THE AUTHOR
Stuart Kallen has written over 80 children's books, including
many environmental science books.

Contents

DOGS AND WOLVES: CLOSE COUSINS

Dogs have been living with humans for more than 12,000 years. Today, hundreds of millions of dogs live in the world. Over 400 **breeds** exist.

All dogs are related to the wolf. Some dogs—like tiny poodles or Great Danes—may look nothing like the wolf. But under their skin, every dog shares many feelings and **traits** with the wolf.

The dog family is called Canidae, from the Latin word meaning "dog." The canid family has 37 **species**, including foxes, jackals, wild dogs, and wolves.

All dogs are related to the wolf.

DALMATIANS

Many **myths** surround the **origins** of the Dalmatian. Old books say these dogs may have come from India, Denmark, France, or Austria. Most experts believe these dogs were **bred** in Dalmatia, a western region in the former Yugoslavia. Dalmatians were named after this region.

In Europe, Dalmatians slept in the stables with the horses and **carriages**. They were called "coach dogs." They ran behind the horse-drawn coaches and protected them from robbers on the highway. At night they guarded the carriage.

In England and America, Dalmatians moved into firehouses with the horse-drawn fire wagons. Firefighters welcomed these useful dogs. When the alarm bell rang, Dalmatians led the fire wagon out of the station. They ran ahead to clear the streets. Once at the fire, the dogs helped find people trapped in burning buildings.

Today, Dalmatians are one of the most popular dog breeds in North America.

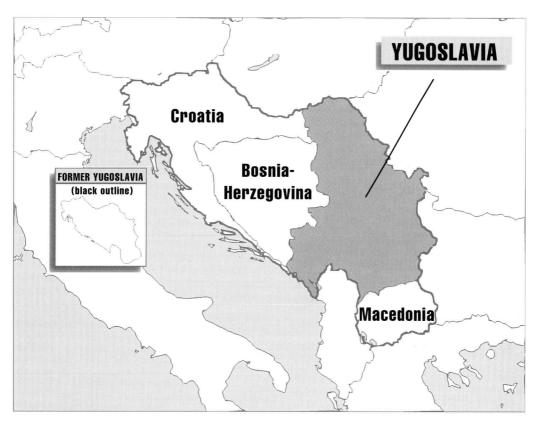

YUGOSLAVIA

Croatia

FORMER YUGOSLAVIA
(black outline)

Bosnia-
Herzegovina

Macedonia

Detail
Area

The name "Dalmatian" came from Dalmatia, a western region in the former Yugoslavia where Croatia exists today.

WHAT THEY'RE LIKE

With their black-and-white spots, Dalmatians look different than any other dog. They are amazing runners. When they run at full stride, their back arches and their hind legs pass their front legs. Having been **bred** to run with **carriages**, Dalmatians can run for hours without tiring.

Dalmatians are smart and even-tempered. They make a fine family pet.

Dalmatians have black-and-white spots that make them look different than all other dogs.

COAT AND COLOR

The Dalmatian's **coat** is thick, hard, fine, and sleek. The black or brown spots are the size of a quarter. A Dalmatian puppy is pure white when it is born. Thick black or liver-brown spots develop at two weeks.

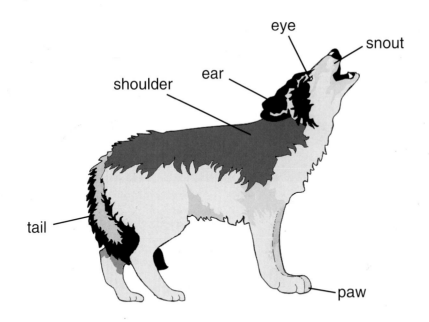

eye

snout

ear

shoulder

tail

paw

All dogs share the same features with their common ancestor, the wolf.

The Dalmatian's coat is thick, hard, fine and sleek.

SIZE

The adult Dalmatian measures about 24 inches (60 cm) from the ground to its shoulders. It weighs 45 to 79 pounds (20 to 36 kg). Its body is lean and long. The Dalmatian's head is long and powerfully built. It has floppy ears set high on its head.

The Dalmatian has floppy ears set high on its head.

CARE

Dalmatians fit in well with most families. They are people-pleasers. If not watched, however, Dalmatians will wander far from home. It is important to have a large yard for a Dalmatian.

Like all dogs, Dalmatians need the same things that humans need: a warm bed, food, water, exercise, and lots of love.

Dalmatians have short hair that needs to be brushed once a week. Sometimes, the dog will need a bath and its nails clipped. All dogs need shots every year. These shots stop diseases such as **distemper** and **hepatitis**.

As a member of your household, your dog expects love and attention. Dalmatians enjoy human contact and like to **retrieve** sticks or catch Frisbees. They need to run and can follow a bicycle for hours.

Dalmatians enjoy human contact and like to retrieve sticks or catch Frisbees.

FEEDING

Like all dogs, Dalmatians eat meat. But Dalmatians need a well-balanced diet. Most dog foods—dry or canned—will give the dog proper **nutrition**.

When you buy a puppy, find out what it has been eating and continue that diet. A small puppy needs four to five small meals a day. By six months, it will need only two meals a day. By one year, a single evening feeding will be enough.

Dalmatians must be exercised every day so they do not gain weight. Walking, running, and playing together will keep you and your dog happy and healthy. Give your dog a hard rubber ball with which to play.

Like any animal, a Dalmatian needs fresh water. Keep water next to the dog's food bowl and change it daily.

*Dalmatians
need a well-
balanced
diet.*

THINGS THEY NEED

Dogs need a quiet place to sleep. A soft dog bed in a quiet corner is the best place for a Dalmatian to sleep. Dalmatians should live indoors. If the dog must live outside, give it a dry, **insulated** dog house.

Dalmatians love to run. A fenced-in yard is the perfect home for the dog. If that is not possible, use a chain on a runner.

In most cities and towns, dogs must be leashed when going for a walk. Dogs also need a license. A dog license has the owner's name, address, and telephone number on it. If the dog runs away, the owners can be called.

Dalmatians love to run and play.

PUPPIES

Average Dalmatians can have up to nine puppies at one time. The dog is **pregnant** for about nine weeks. When she is ready to give birth, she needs a dark place away from noises. If your dog is pregnant, give her a strong box lined with an old blanket. She will have her puppies there.

Puppies are tiny and helpless when born. They arrive about half an hour apart. The mother licks them clean which helps them start breathing. Their eyes are shut, making them blind for their first nine days. They are also deaf for about ten days.

Dogs are **mammals**. They drink milk from their mother. After four weeks, puppies will grow teeth. Separate the puppies from their mother and give them soft dog food.

Dalmatians have up to nine puppies at a time.

GLOSSARY

BREED - A grouping of animals with the same traits.

CARRIAGE (KAIR-ij) - A vehicle that moves on wheels and is pulled by horses.

COAT - The dog's outer covering (hair).

DISTEMPER - A contagious disease of dogs and certain other animals, caused by a virus.

HEPATITIS (hep-uh-TIE-tis) - An inflammation of the liver caused by a virus.

INSULATION (in-sue-LAY-shun) - Something that stops heat loss.

MAMMAL - A group of animals, including humans, that have hair and feed their young milk.

MYTH - A story.

NUTRITION (new-TRISH-un) - Food; nourishment.

ORIGIN - A beginning or starting point.

PREGNANT - With one or more babies growing inside the body.

RETRIEVE - To return or bring back.

SPECIES (SPEE-seas) - A kind or type.

TRAIT - A characteristic or feature of the animal.

Index

BIBLIOGRAPHY

American Kennel Club. *The Complete Dog Book*. New York: Macmillan, 1992.

Clutton-Brock, Juliet. *Dog*. New York: Alfred A. Knopf, 1991.

The Complete Book of the Dog. New York: Holt, Rinehart, & Winston, 1985.

Ditto, Tanya B. *Dalmatians*. Hauppauge, NY: Barron's Educational Series, 1991.

Sylvester, Patricia. *The Reader's Digest Illustrated Book of Dogs*. New York: The Reader's Digest Association, 1984.